THE GREAT MISCONCEPTION

Angels, Demons, Satan and The Underworld

DR OSCAR GUOBADIA

Published by Dr Oscar Guobadia

Printed in the United Kingdom

THE GREAT MISCONCEPTION © 2020 by DR OSCAR GUOBADIA

All rights reserved.

Under International Copyright Law, no part of this publication may be reproduced, stored, or transmitted by any means – electronic, mechanical, photographic [Photocopy], recording, or otherwise – without written permission from the publisher.

The right of DR OSCAR GUOBADIA to be identified as the author of this work has been asserted by him in accordance with the Copyright, Designs and Patents Act 1988 and any subsequent amendments thereof.

All Scripture quotations, unless otherwise indicated, are taken from the Authorised King James Version® Scripture quotations from The Authorised [KJV] Version.

Rights in the NKJV in the United Kingdom are vested in the Crown. Reproduced by permission of Crown's patentee, Cambridge University Press.

ISBN – 9798673053836

DEDICATION

I dedicate this book to my beautiful Mom Rita, who has been an amazing woman and has always spoken life and prayed for me. I watched how she spent all she had to ensure I had the best of what I have. Words really fail me to express my profound gratitude to this woman. My prayer for you is to always keep loving and caring for people as you've always done.

As I write these words about Angels, I am almost tempted to call you one because you are nothing short of extraordinarily beautiful. I love you mom and I really honour you, your strength, courage and dedication.

All these and more because you still believe there's more in me.

Table of contents

Foreword 1
Introduction 3
Angels 8
Ministry Of Angels 14
The Major Players 24
Super Angels 38
The Four Faces Before The Throne Of God 44
The Misconceptions Of Satan 47
The Hybrids 59
Demons 61
Demonology 66
Closing Remark 76

FOREWORD

God shares inside information with His prophetic vessels. There is nothing more exciting than to sit at the feet of a person who has been with Jesus and is expounding His mind. Prophets and prophetic people are called to expose, reveal, and help to dismantle demonic schemes and structures.

> *"See, I have this day set thee over the nations and over the kingdoms, to root out, and to pull down, and to destroy, and to throw down, to build, and to plant"* — Jer. 1:10

This is a part of the charge that God gave to Jeremiah as a prophet. I have always believed that prophets in the New Covenant are foundational in God's government on the earth and in the Kingdom building apparatus. When they are labouring alongside of apostles, there is a highly effective building team that sees, knows, reveals, and establishes. The prophetic grace empowers the apostolic by releasing Kingdom insight and revelation. Demonic rulers and structures are exposed as the authority of the Lord is released to tear them down.

The dimension of prophetic warfare often brings heavy personal attacks for prophets, prophetic people, and prophetic assemblies. This is the reason they need strong teaching to develop a root system that sustains them in the midst of attack.

It is rare to find a person with deep theological understanding, breathtaking prophetic gifting, and solid apostolic function. Dr. Oscar Guobadia is such a person. In this writing, you will find layer upon layer of revelation to arm you for the days ahead. Your prophetic stamina will be increased and the mind of the Lord will be revealed to you.

This is a serious read for serious warriors and lovers of Jesus. It is a vital tool in the hands of the sent ones. It is a battle cry and a road map. As you read these pages, prepare to be both challenged and equipped! Let's go!

Ryan LeStrange

Author of #1 New Release on Amazon,
Hell's Toxic Trio and other titles

INTRODUCTION

One would almost wonder why I have decided to write a book on Angels, demons, Satan, hell and the underworld, seeing that there are countless volumes of this topic from different theological perspectives.

Non-faith organisations also have their views on the topic of Angels and demons. Honestly, I have literally wondered why there are less sound biblical and theological teachings in this area but then again, I realised because most preachers are not comfortable with the reality of these conversation, others deny some facts or do not want to touch this area.

If we ask the average believer where is Heaven, they are quick to point the sky beyond the clouds, gazing pass the galaxies and in utter amazement say "above the firmament". Oh, you'd also be surprised that the same people would point the ground and say "Well, if Heaven is further up, then hell is under the earth". I think this group of people are in a better understanding than the rest of the saints who believe Heaven is a reality but at the same time say hell is only a figure of speech. And in their theological position is "We cannot have a good God who created a bad place for us to stay for eternity" but each time I point to them that God never intended for man to end up in Hell, it all ends up an uproar…. Hell was made for satan and his demons!

"When He had come to the other side, to the country of the Gergesenes, there met Him two demon-possessed men, coming out of the tombs, exceedingly fierce, so that no one could pass that way. And suddenly they

cried out, saying, "What have we to do with You, Jesus, You Son of God? Have You come here to torment us before the time?" - Matthew 8:28-29

Their place of eternal torment is in hell, thus they questioned if Jesus had come to send them to hell before the time. This is one of the many reasons we believe the eternal destiny of satan and his minions will be in hell as an everlasting punishment

After giving an exhaustive teaching about the end of the age, the coming judgement and destruction of Jerusalem in 70AD in Matthew 24, Jesus made a statement in the following chapter when the Son of man judge the nation in chapter twenty five about the Sheep and Goat judgement said:

*"Then He will also say to those on the left hand, Depart from Me, you cursed, into the everlasting fire **prepared for the devil and his angels**" - Matthew 25:41*

You see Jesus reaffirming that hell was never His intention for man but His justice demands that there is a penalty for sin but at the same time offered a redemptive plan for man by offering Himself as the perfect sacrifice for sin.

*"The Lord is not slack concerning His promise, as some count slackness, but is longsuffering toward us, **not willing that any should perish but that all should come to repentance**" - 2 Peter 3:9*

His desire is that we spend eternity with Him in paradise, not torment with Satan and demons in hell.

In my opinion, we haven't done a good teaching the saints the boundaries of our reality and the reality outside our boundaries. We think this is all there is to life. We have made the earth our habitation instead of our destination. We are pilgrims on a journey and someday, we'll get to our destination where we'll be with our father. The writer to the Hebrews gave an amazing exhortation to the persecuted believers in those days when he said:

"for he waited for the city which has foundations, whose builder and maker is God". - "Hebrews 11:10

What City you may ask. The writer went on in the next chapter to explain to us:

"But you have come to Mount Zion and to the city of the living God, the heavenly Jerusalem, to an innumerable company of angels, 23 to the general assembly and church of the firstborn who are registered in heaven, to God the Judge of all, to the spirits of just men made perfect, 24 to Jesus the Mediator of the new covenant, and to the blood of sprinkling that speaks better things than that of Abel". - Hebrews 12:22-24

He calls it Mount Zion, the heavenly Jerusalem, not the one in Tel Aviv but the one that is in Heaven, as he concludes in the next chapter that this present one will cease to continue at some point.

"For here we have no continuing city, but we seek the one to come. 15 Therefore by Him let us continually offer the sacrifice of praise to God, that is, the fruit of our lips, giving thanks to His name".- Hebrews 13:14-15

You can see that God's desire for us is to be with Him in paradise and that is what Christ has gone to do in Heaven – To go prepare a place for us. He is still preparing but almost done and once He's done, He's definitely coming for us as He promised us in John 14

"Let not your heart be troubled; you believe in God, believe also in Me. 2 In My Father's house are many mansions; if it were not so, I would have told you. I go to prepare a place for you. And if I go and prepare a place for you, I will come again and receive you to Myself; that where I am, there you may be also. And where I go you know, and the way you know."

- John 14:1-4

This is our glorious hope – knowing that this part of life on the earth is only temporal and we are looking forward to that blessed hope!

"looking for the blessed hope and glorious appearing of our great God and Saviour Jesus Christ" - Titus 2:13

Sadly, we have been wired to think that life is all about sleeping and waking up, going to Church and doing life, acquiring treasure on this part of life and nothing about living for God. And in our minds eyes, we die and go to heaven. God wants us to be aware of certain things on this part of life – you could say certain spiritual realities that influences decisions, government, systems on this part of life. Truth is that until we come to realise that we live in an artificial simulation, we'll struggle living all that the Lord has called us to live on the earth. There is a reality outside the bound of time, space and matter – There is a dimension we are yet to unravel. This is not taught in many Churches, while others fear exposing believers to this reality. I really do not want to sound spooky but suffice to say that there is a real world with real events with real conversations happening concurrently as the one we are currently in.

Many Christians are unaware of the activities of Angels, Demons and some supernatural encounters, and this has robbed us the privilege of engaging these realms, thereby reverencing God's majestic handiwork. What we fail to realise is that there are powers controlling things on this part of life and sooner we understand this, the better we start praying. Many Christians do not understand that they'd have to win certain battles in the spiritual realm before they can claim their breakthrough here on this part of life. This is the reason I had done an extensive work explaining with biblical texts these realities of Angels and demons as well as their limitations. It is my deepest desire that the Body of Christ come to the full knowledge and understanding of these dimensions and learn to approach these realms. All through scripture, we read of demonic encounters but we have been unable to press in to investigate their origin, their assignment and their future – This is the reason why many believers are unable to win life's war.

In this book, I was emphatic on the distinctions between Angels, demons, Hell, Satan, the underworld, etc. I believe this book will challenge you to appreciate the integrity of the Bible and of course honour the author of the Holy Scriptures.

Finally, I'd like to mention on here that Angels, demons, Satan, hell and the underworld are not abstracts but a reality we must come to study and understand in order to grasp the wealth if the scripture and appropriate them for daily Christian living. It is my prayer that you enjoy this book and I hope it blesses you.

Thank you

Dr Oscar Guobadia

ANGELS

All through scripture, we are faced with all kind of events about the supernatural realms, supernatural beings and their eternal destinations. I am always fascinated by these encounters and how they serve God's eternal purpose.

I have always questioned the realities of the supernatural dimension until I became privy of the scope and the reality that God is a creator, which means that He was deliberate about dimensions when He carved out realms and planes. The constellation realm is real and we've seen scripture unfold as we press in for a holistic Bible commitment.

May I put this out there before we dive deep. I believe in angelic ministry and an avid believer that they engage with us on daily basis. However, I am not in support of the excessive exaggeration of angelic ministries for personal errands. They complete ownership of angels and the thought of commanding them at will is not scriptural and these teachings needs to be readdressed. teachings

For instance, Paul made a strange remark when admonishing the Corinthian brethren.

"It is doubtless not profitable for me to boast. I will come to visions and revelations of the Lord: I know a man in Christ who fourteen years ago— whether in the body I do not know, or whether out of the body I do not

know, God knows—such a one was caught up to the third heaven. And I know such a man—whether in the body or out of the body I do not know, God knows— how he was caught up into Paradise and heard inexpressible words, which it is not lawful for a man to utter". – 2 Corinthians 12:1-4

From this scripture, we can infer that the first Heaven is the atmosphere, the second Heaven is the constellation dimension or the stellar heaven which includes the sun, the moon, the stars and the third heaven Is the Throne of God.

This takes us back to Paul's admonition to the Ephesian brethren when he encouraged them to put on the whole armour of God in order to contend with spiritual forces. What we may not realise is that the spiritual realms are the constellation realm and the throne of God.

The material world where we live is highly influenced by activities in the supernatural realm, but what we need to realise is that we need to war from God's realm in order to win the war against powers in the stellar heaven.

Before we address Angelic and demonic beings, we need to be clear about the realms that they exist in. Demons and fallen angels have locality just as we do, their genetic design is made for the realms that they exist in. We are humans and our genetic makeup is built to adapt with earth's ecological design, which means that in order for these celestial beings in the constellation plane to respond to earth's design, they need to have a characteristic known as *adaptation*.

The Apostle Paul in 1 Corinthians 15 was addressing the Corinthian believers about our final victory when he said:

"Now this I say, brethren, that flesh and blood cannot inherit the kingdom of God; nor does corruption inherit incorruption. Behold, I tell you a mystery: We shall not all sleep, but we shall all be changed— in a

moment, in the twinkling of an eye, at the last trumpet. For the trumpet will sound, and the dead will be raised incorruptible, and we shall be changed. For this corruptible must put on incorruption, and this mortal must put on immortality. So when this corruptible has put on incorruption, and this mortal has put on immortality, then shall be brought to pass the saying that is written: "Death is swallowed up in victory." - 1 Cor 15:50-54

According to the text, The Paul didn't imply that "material things cannot inherit the kingdom of God," because we know Jesus' resurrection body was very much a body as He mentioned when He appeared before the Apostles

"Behold My hands and My feet, that it is I Myself. Handle Me and see, for a spirit does not have flesh and bones as you see I have." - Luke 24:39

He first says to them "Behold". The word in the Greek is *eido* which means to see. The word for handle is *pselaphao,* which means to touch or feel. Jesus was seen, and touched which conforms that His body has to be material. Someone once asked me why flesh and bones, where is the blood, and I said He shed all on the cross for all mankind!

Then Paul went on to say that our physical bodies are subject to diseases and will someday decay, but heaven cannot decay away. Heaven is incorrupt. This present bodies we have on cannot inherit the incorruptible Heaven. Then to further buttress his point, he gave them a mystery – This means that it can only be interpreted spiritually. He mentions that we shall not all sleep but that we shall all be changed. We know that death is not used in the New Testament of a believer who passes, instead sleep is used! There are some people that will not face physical death but everyone shall be changed at the return of Jesus.

Many people think that the Apostle missed the eschatological timeline, but I believe that epistle was addressing the believers in his day and us today, but most importantly, he lived his life believing and expecting the return of the Lord. Therefore, his writing points to Jesus imminent return and he [Paul] never gave us the exact time for the return of Christ.

When the Lord shall appear, the dead will be raised incorruptible, and we shall be changed if we are alive at His coming: In a single moment, Jesus will gather His people both dead and on the earth to Himself for resurrection.

The apostle Paul uses the word rapture here to mean "Caught up" as seen when he wrote to the believers in Thessalonica.

"For this we say to you by the word of the Lord, that we who are alive and remain until the coming of the Lord will by no means precede those who are asleep. For the Lord Himself will descend from heaven with a shout, with the voice of an archangel, and with the trumpet of God. And the dead in Christ will rise first. Then we who are alive and remain shall be caught up together with them in the clouds to meet the Lord in the air. And thus we shall always be with the Lord. Therefore comfort one another with these words" - *"1 Thessalonians 4:15-18*

It is often believed that the last trumpet was a figure of speech that came from the Roman military, when they broke camp.

They believe that the first trumpet meant, "strike the tents and prepare to leave" The second trumpet meant, "fall into line". The third and last trumpet meant "march away."

This last trumpet describes the Christian's "marching orders" at the rapture of the Church.

Therefore we can say that this corruptible must put on incorruption, which is also called the Glorification body!

Our bodies cannot inherit or gain access to a Heaven, but in order for us to do this, we need *adaptation*. This adaptation is a technical term referred to as Glorification. We need to put on or wear an incorrupt body which enables us function in that Kingdom.

This is important because it gives us our boundaries of reality. It also gives Angelic and demonic beings their boundaries of operation and as we journey on, we'll see their limitations on the earth.

We'll be discussing the characteristics and limitations that we know from the truths of the bible. We'll also be addressing the specific major players we encounter in the bible, not fictions, not literatures, not the little silly things we read on Christmas cards or renaissance art, and so forth, but the reality of these creatures that are incredibly powerful and are there to minister to us strangely enough.

We will not rely on occult literatures and non-biblical sources that pervades our libraries but there are ancient records that supports the concepts of the Nephilim – These strange hybrids of the past we encountered in Genesis 6.

Every major culture deals with this, but we'll use the Holy Bible as our source of information that uniquely confirmed itself by the fact that it can demonstrate that its origin is from an extra-terrestrial origin, meaning the source has to be supernatural. We cannot tackle supernatural beings and take the risk not use the Bible as our inspiration and source.

In this book as we look at Angels, we'll talk about their capabilities, limitations, we'll also address some super Angels- Cherubim, Seraphim, Guardian Angels, and so on. I know many of you think that that Guardian Angels are nursery traditions, but it turns out that they are actually biblical.

"The angel of the Lord encamps all around those who fear Him, And delivers them". - Ps 34:7

We'll also address the major star players such as Gabriel who is the Messianic angel and Michael who is the war angel.

The word Angel in the Hebrew is known as Mal'ak, which means one who is dispatched with a message. That term Is used a hundred and ninety-six times in the scriptures.

Hundred and eleven times it is referred to as angels in the sense of a supernatural messenger of some kind and ninety-eight times, it's just a messenger. It is used forty-four times used as ambassadors.

As you do your own study, you'll realise that the term has its own ambiguity.

In the Greek, both in the OT and the NT, the word is Aggelos which means a messenger, an envoy, one who is sent implicitly from God.

A hundred and seventy-nine times translated as angels, seven times just as messengers.

The seven letters to the seven churches make references to this, but some scholars think it's just a name for the pastor of those Churches, but most scholars ascribe a supernatural role to them

MINISTRY OF ANGELS

1. CONTINUALLY SERVE THOSE WHO WILL INHERIT SALVATION

"Are they not all ministering spirits sent forth to minister for those who will inherit salvation"? – Hebrews 1:14

If you are one of those, the angels are there to serve you whether you realise this or not. They are real, it's not just a euphemism or a cliché, they are very live and real.

2. THEY REVEAL UNKNOWN TRUTHS

Now I have come to make you understand what will happen to your people in the latter days, for the vision refers to many days yet to come."

When he had spoken such words to me, I turned my face toward the ground and became speechless. And suddenly, one having the likeness of the sons of men touched my lips; then I opened my mouth and spoke, saying to him who stood before me, "My lord, because of the vision my sorrows have overwhelmed me, and I have retained no strength. For how can this servant of my lord talk with you, my lord? As for me, no strength remains in me now, nor is any breath left in me." Then again, the one having the likeness of a man touched me and strengthened me. And he said, "O man greatly beloved, fear not! Peace be to you; be strong, yes, be strong!" So when he spoke to me I was strengthened, and said, "Let my lord speak, for you have strengthened me." Then he said, "Do you know why I have come to you? And now I must return to fight with the prince of Persia; and when I have gone forth, indeed the prince of Greece will come. But I will tell you what is noted in the Scripture of Truth. (No one upholds me against these, except Michael your prince. - Daniel 10:14-21

"For there stood by me this night an angel of the God to whom I belong and whom I serve, saying, 'Do not be afraid, Paul; you must be brought before Caesar; and indeed God has granted you all those who sail with you. Therefore take heart, men, for I believe God that it will be just as it was told me. However, we must run aground on a certain island." - Acts 27:23-26

There are number of places where angels revealed something you didn't know before.

3. THEY GIVE PRSONAL GUIDANCE

But while he thought about these things, behold, an angel of the Lord appeared to him in a dream, saying, "Joseph, son of David, do not be afraid to take to you Mary your wife, for that which is conceived in her is of the Holy Spirit. And she will bring forth a Son, and you shall call His name Jesus, for He will save His people from their sins. - Matthew 1:20-21

Now there were in the same country shepherds living out in the fields, keeping watch over their flock by night. And behold, an angel of the Lord stood before them, and the glory of the Lord shone around them, and they were greatly afraid. Then the angel said to them, "Do not be afraid, for behold, I bring you good tidings of great joy which will be to all people. For there is born to you this day in the city of David a Saviour, who is

Christ the Lord. And this will be the sign to you: You will find a Babe wrapped in swaddling clothes, lying in a manger." - Luke 2:8-12

4. THEY PROTCT YOU FROM HARM

There are cases where you are protected from harm even without realising "My God sent His angel and shut the lions' mouths, so that they have not hurt me, because I was found innocent before Him; and also, O king, I have done no wrong before you."- Daniel 6:22

5. THY DELIVER US FROM OUR ENEMIES

But at night an angel of the Lord opened the prison doors and brought them out, and said, "Go, stand in the temple and speak to the people all the words of this life." And when they heard that, they entered the temple early in the morning and taught. But the high priest and those with him came and called the council together, with all the elders of the children of Israel, and sent to the prison to have them brought. - Acts 5:19-21

Now behold, an angel of the Lord stood by him, and a light shone in the prison; and he struck Peter on the side and raised him up, saying, "Arise quickly!" And his chains fell off his hands. Then the angel said to him, "Gird yourself and tie on your sandals"; and so he did. And he said to him, "Put on your garment and follow me." So, he went out and followed him, and did not know that what was done by the angel was real, but thought he was seeing a vision. When they were past the first and the second guard posts, they came to the iron gate that leads to the city, which opened to them of its own accord; and they went out and went down one street, and immediately the angel departed from him. And when Peter had come to himself, he said, "Now I know for certain that the Lord has sent His angel, and has delivered me from the hand of Herod and from all the expectation of the Jewish people." - Acts 12:7-11

6. WE SEE ANGELS STRENGTHERS AND ENCOURAGERS:

(a)-Jacob was encouraged

"So Jacob went on his way, and the angels of God met him. 2 When Jacob saw them, he said, "This is God's camp." And he called the name of that place Mahanaim". - Genesis 32:1-2

(b)-Daniel was encouraged all through the book of Daniel

Then it happened, when I, Daniel, had seen the vision and was seeking the meaning, that suddenly there stood before me one having the appearance of a man. And I heard a man's voice between the banks of the Ulai, who called, and said, "Gabriel, make this man understand the vision." So he came near where I stood, and when he came, I was afraid and fell on my face; but he said to me, "Understand, son of man, that the vision refers to the time of the end." - Daniel 8:15-17

(c)- Suddenly, a hand touched me, which made me tremble on my knees and on the palms of my hands. And he said to me, "O Daniel, man greatly beloved, understand the words that I speak to you, and stand upright, for I have now been sent to you." While he was speaking this word to me, I stood trembling". - Daniel 10:10-11

(d)- Paul had frequent encounters with angels

"For there stood by me this night an angel of the God to whom I belong and whom I serve, 24 saying, 'Do not be afraid, Paul; you must be brought before Caesar; and indeed God has granted you all those who sail with you.' - Acts 27:23-24

(e)- They provided food for Elijah back

"And when he saw that, he arose and ran for his life, and went to Beersheba, which belongs to Judah, and left his servant there. But he himself went a day's journey into the wilderness, and came and sat down under a broom tree. And he prayed that he might die, and said, "It is enough! Now, Lord, take my life, for I am no better than my fathers!" Then as he lay and slept under a broom tree, suddenly an angel touched him, and said to him, "Arise and eat." Then he looked, and there by his head was a cake baked on coals, and a jar of water. So he ate and drank, and lay down again. And the angel of the Lord came back the second time, and touched him, and said, "Arise and eat, because the journey is too great for you." 8 So he arose, and ate and drank; and he went in the strength of that food forty days and forty nights as far as Horeb, the mountain of God". - 1 Kings 19:3-8

We see them all through the bible ministering, helping, providing, shielding, strengthening. Their ministry may be invisible, but it sure has tangible results.

7. THEY GUIDE US

"When the morning dawned, the angels urged Lot to hurry, saying, "Arise, take your wife and your two daughters who are here, lest you be consumed in the punishment of the city." And while he lingered, the men took hold of his hand, his wife's hand, and the hands of his two daughters, the Lord being merciful to him, and they brought him out and set him outside the city. So it came to pass, when they had brought them outside, that he said, "Escape for your life! Do not look behind you nor stay anywhere in the plain. Escape to the mountains, lest you be destroyed." - Genesis 19:15-17

8. THEY DELIVER US

"Now behold, an angel of the Lord stood by him, and a light shone in the prison; and he struck Peter on the side and raised him up, saying, "Arise quickly!" And his chains fell off his hands". - Acts 12:7

9. THEY ENLIGHTEN US

Now when Herod was dead, behold, an angel of the Lord appeared in a dream to Joseph in Egypt, saying, "Arise, take the young Child and His mother, and go to the land of Israel, for those who sought the young Child's life are dead." - Matthew 2:19-20

10. THEY EMPOWER US

Then an angel appeared to Him from heaven, strengthening Him. - Luke 22:43

11. THEY PROTECT US

For He shall give His angels charge over you, To keep you in all your ways. In their hands they shall bear you up, Lest you dash your foot against a stone.- Psalms 91:11-12

This protection thing can be very real.

I suspect that many times, we are beneficiaries of angels we are not even aware of, we only realise when we study and know that it was part of God's purpose for us.

Angels are not abstractions or concepts; they are personal beings meaning:

12. THEY HAVE INTELLECT

And behold, there was a great earthquake; for an angel of the Lord descended from heaven, and came and rolled back the stone from the door, and sat on it- Matthew 28:2

To them it was revealed that, not to themselves, but to us they were ministering the things which now have been reported to you through those who have preached the gospel to you by the Holy Spirit sent from heaven—things which angels desire to look into- 1 Peter 1:12

13. THEY HAVE EMOTIONS

When the morning stars sang together, And all the sons of God shouted for joy? - Job 38:7

Likewise, I say to you, there is joy in the presence of the angels of God over one sinner who repents."- Luke 15:10

14. THEY HAVE WILL, THEY MAKE CHOICES

And the angels who did not keep their proper domain, but left their own abode, He has reserved in everlasting chains under darkness for the judgment of the great day; - Jude 1:6

They can make bad choices and we'll discover the results of some of the angel's bad choices as we go further in this study

Not only are they personal, they are also spirit beings, which means that:

They are not limited to material bodies – Heb. 1:14

Are they not all ministering spirits sent forth to minister for those who will inherit salvation? - Hebrews 1:14. They are distinctive in that they can materialise but they are not limited to what we consider a material body

An angel can only be in one place at one time. This is because they are not like God who is omnipresent. They have locality

yes, while I was speaking in prayer, the man Gabriel, whom I had seen in the vision at the beginning, being caused to fly swiftly, reached me about the time of the evening offering. 22 And he informed me, and talked with me, and said, "O Daniel, I have now come forth to give you skill to understand. 23 At the beginning of your supplications the command went out, and I have come to tell you, for you are greatly beloved; therefore consider the matter, and understand the vision- Daniel 9:21-23

When we see them, they appear in the form of men, sometimes in natural sight with human functions – [Gen 18:1-22, 19:1]. Sometimes angels are seen by some and not others

And when the servant of the man of God arose early and went out, there was an army, surrounding the city with horses and chariots. And his servant said to him, "Alas, my master! What shall we do?" So he answered, "Do not fear, for those who are with us are more than those who are with them." And Elisha prayed, and said, "Lord, I pray, open his eyes that he may see." Then the Lord opened the eyes of the young man, and he saw. And behold, the mountain was full of horses and chariots of fire all around Elisha- 2 Kings 6:15-17

Angels do not reproduce –For when they rise from the dead, they neither marry nor are given in marriage, but are like angels in heaven. - Mark 12:25

Angels do not die –nor can they die anymore, for they are equal to the angels and are sons of God, being sons of the resurrection. - Luke 20:36

They can engage in reproductive mischief as seen in Gen 6

"Now it came to pass, when men began to multiply on the face of the earth, and daughters were born to them, 2 that the sons of God saw the daughters of men, that they were beautiful; and they took wives for themselves of all whom they chose".- Genesis 6:1-2

They do have physical realities:

They lead people by the hand

When the morning dawned, the angels urged Lot to hurry, saying, "Arise, take your wife and your two daughters who are here, lest you be consumed in the punishment of the city."- Genesis 19:15

They indulge in combat – 2 Kings 19:35 [Read 2Kings 19 where they slaughtered a hundred and eighty-five Syrians] – Sennacherib, king of Syria never ever attacked Israel again after that. They had previously wiped out the northern kingdom but God protected the southern kingdom. We are told in the NT that many of us have entertained angels unaware

Do not forget to entertain strangers, for by so doing some have unwittingly entertained angel - Hebrews 13:2.

We could mistake them as people, it is a capability they have

Angels have attributes in the degree greater than men but less than God

- They have more knowledge than men [Matt 244:31, Luke 1:13-16. But less than God – [Matt 24:35]
- They have more power than men but less than God.
- We need to understand that on one hand their reality but also sensitive to their limitations

Angels are organised and ranked; they are not random individuals on assignment.

There's only one arch angel in the bible – Michael

Yet Michael the archangel, in contending with the devil, when he disputed about the body of Moses, dared not bring against him a reviling accusation, but said, "The Lord rebuke you!"- Jude 1:9

There are also chief princes:

But the prince of the kingdom of Persia withstood me twenty-one days; and behold, Michael, one of the chief princes, came to help me, for I had been left alone there with the kings of Persia. - Daniel 10:13

There is a certain kind of Angels called Cherubim

Then the Lord God said, "Behold, the man has become like one of Us, to know good and evil. And now, lest he put out his hand and take also of the tree of life, and eat, and live forever"— 23 therefore the Lord God sent him out of the garden of Eden to till the ground from which he was taken. 24 So He drove out the man; and He placed cherubim at the east of the garden of Eden, and a flaming sword which turned every way, to guard the way to the tree of life. - Genesis 3:22-24

A Cherub biblically is not a little chubby baby with wings often characterised in renaissance art. That's a fictional concept. Cherubim were assigned to guard the way to the tree of life when Adam was kicked out of the garden. One of the Cherubim was in-charge of all the rest and got carried away on ego trip, and we know that one satan. He'll be a special focus as we move along

We also encountered a special kind in the book of Isaiah known as *seraphim – a flaming one* of some kind

In the year that King Uzziah died, I saw the Lord sitting on a throne, high and lifted up, and the train of His robe filled the temple. Above it stood seraphim; each one had six wings: with two he covered his face, with two he covered his feet, and with two he flew. And one cried to another and said: "Holy, holy, holy is the Lord of hosts; The whole earth is full of His glory!"- Isaiah 6:1-3

The word itself implies a source of light, a source of brightness. It was only mentioned in Isaiah 6, but it was also synonymous to the creatures in Revelation 4

In Revelation 4, we find living creatures defined.

THE MAJOR PLAYERS

THE ANGEL OF THE LORD [THEOPHANIES]

Most scholars infer that those references are not angels but are an Old Testament appearance of Jesus Christ before His incarnation. It's very important we discuss about Him because what we know from the bible goes way above what we know about angels.

THE ANGEL OF THE LORD IN THE BIBLE:

To Hagar - she identifies Him as the Lord – Gen 16:7-14

Now the Angel of the Lord found her by a spring of water in the wilderness, by the spring on the way to Shur. And He said, "Hagar, Sarai's maid, where have you come from, and where are you going?" She said, "I am fleeing from the presence of my mistress Sarai. " The Angel of the Lord said to her, "Return to your mistress, and submit yourself under her hand." Then the Angel of the Lord said to her, "I will multiply your descendants exceedingly, so that they shall not be counted for multitude." And the Angel of the Lord said to her: "Behold, you are with child,

And you shall bear a son. You shall call his name Ishmael, Because the Lord has heard your affliction. He shall be a wild man; His hand shall be against every man,

And every man's hand against him. And he shall dwell in the presence of all his brethren." Then she called the name of the Lord who spoke to her, You-Are-the-God-Who-Sees; for she said, "Have I also here seen Him who sees me?" Therefore the well was called Beer Lahai Roi; observe, it is between Kadesh and Bered.

To Abraham -When the birth of Isaac was announced in Gen 18

Then the Lord appeared to him by the terebinth trees of Mamre, as he was sitting in the tent door in the heat of the day. So he lifted his eyes and looked, and behold, three men were standing by him; and when he saw them, he ran from the tent door to meet them, and bowed himself to the ground,

To Abraham when he was about to sacrifice Isaac in Gen 22:9-19

Then they came to the place of which God had told him. And Abraham built an altar there and placed the wood in order; and he bound Isaac his son and laid him on the altar, upon the wood. And Abraham stretched out his hand and took the knife to slay his son. But the Angel of the Lord called to him from heaven and said, "Abraham, Abraham!" he said, "Here I am." And He said, "Do not lay your hand on the lad, or do anything to him; for now I know that you fear God, since you have not withheld your son, your only son, from Me." Then Abraham lifted his eyes and looked, and there behind him was a ram caught in a thicket by its horns. So Abraham went and took the ram, and offered it up for a burnt offering instead of his son. And Abraham called the name of the place, The-Lord-Will-Provide; as it is said to this day, "In the Mount of the Lord it shall be provided." Then the Angel of the Lord called to Abraham a second time out of heaven, and said: "By Myself I have sworn, says the Lord, because you have done this thing, and have not withheld your son, your only son blessing I will bless you, and multiplying I will multiply your descendants as the stars of the heaven and as the sand which is on the seashore; and your descendants shall possess the gate of their enemies. In your seed all the nations of the earth shall be blessed, because you have obeyed My voice." So Abraham returned to his young men, and they rose and went together to Beersheba; and Abraham dwelt at Beersheba.

To Jacob - He wrestles with an Angel until he got his blessings - Gen 31

To Moses at the burning bush – Exo 3:6 – We get the impression from John 8 that Jesus identifies Himself as the voice from the burning bush and I AM statements given in Exodus 3 and 4

"Moreover He said, "I am the God of your father—the God of Abraham, the God of Isaac, and the God of Jacob." And Moses hid his face, for he was afraid to look upon God."

To Israel – He led out of Egypt – Exo 14:19

And the Angel of God, who went before the camp of Israel, moved and went behind them; and the pillar of cloud went from before them and stood behind them.

To Israel – He led out of the wilderness – Exo 23:20-23

"Behold, I send an Angel before you to keep you in the way and to bring you into the place which I have prepared. Beware of Him and obey His voice; do not provoke Him, for He will not pardon your transgressions; for My name is in Him. But if you indeed obey His voice and do all that I speak, then I will be an enemy to your enemies and an adversary to your adversaries. For My Angel will go before you and bring you in to the Amorites and the Hittites and the Perizzites and the Canaanites and the Hivites and the Jebusites; and I will cut them off."

To Balaam and his talking donkey - Num. 22:22-35

Then God's anger was aroused because he went, and the Angel of the Lord took His stand in the way as an adversary against him. And he was riding on his donkey, and his two servants were with him. Now the donkey saw the Angel of the Lord standing in the way with His drawn sword in His hand, and the donkey turned aside out of the way and went into the field. So Balaam struck the donkey to turn her back onto the road. Then the Angel of the Lord stood in a narrow path between the vineyards, with a wall on this side and a wall on that side. And when the donkey saw the Angel of the Lord, she pushed herself against the wall and crushed Balaam's foot against the wall; so he struck her again. Then the Angel of the Lord went further, and stood in a narrow place where there was no way to turn either to the right hand or to the left. And when the donkey saw the Angel of the Lord, she lay down under Balaam; so Balaam's anger was aroused, and he struck the donkey with his staff. Then the Lord opened the mouth of the donkey, and she said to Balaam, "What have I done to you, that you have struck me these three times?" And Balaam said to the donkey, "Because you have abused me. I wish there were a sword in my hand, for now I would kill you!" So the donkey said to Balaam, "Am I not your donkey on which you have ridden, ever since I became yours, to this day? Was I ever disposed to do this to you? And he said, "No." Then the Lord opened Balaam's eyes, and he saw the Angel of the Lord standing in the way with His drawn sword in His hand; and he bowed his head and fell flat on his face. And the Angel of the Lord said to him, "Why have you struck your donkey these three times? Behold, I have come out to stand against you, because your way is perverse before Me. The donkey saw Me and turned aside from Me these three times. If she had not turned aside from Me, surely I would also have killed you by now, and let her live." And Balaam said to the Angel of the Lord, "I have sinned, for I did not know You stood in the way against me. Now therefore, if it displeases You, I will turn back." Then the Angel of the Lord said to Balaam, "Go with the men, but only the word that I speak to you, that you shall speak." So Balaam went with the princes of Balak.

To Joshua as he approaches Jericho – Joshua 5:13-15

And it came to pass, when Joshua was by Jericho, that he lifted his eyes and looked, and behold, a Man stood opposite him with His sword drawn in His hand. And Joshua went to Him and said to Him, "Are You for us or for our adversaries?" So He said, "No, but as Commander of the army of the Lord I have now come." And Joshua fell on his face to the earth and worshiped, and said to Him, "What does my Lord say to His servant?" Then the Commander of the Lord's army said to Joshua, "Take your sandal off your foot, for the place where you stand is holy." And Joshua did so.

Gideon's call as a judge – Judges 6

Now the Angel of the Lord came and sat under the terebinth tree which was in Ophrah, which belonged to Joash the Abiezrite, while his son Gideon threshed wheat in the winepress, in order to hide it from the Midianites. And the Angel of the Lord appeared to him, and said to him, "The Lord is with you, you mighty man of valour!" Gideon said to Him, "O my lord, if the Lord is with us, why then has all this happened to us? And where are all His miracles which our fathers told us about, saying, 'Did not the Lord bring us up from Egypt?' But now the Lord has forsaken us and delivered us into the hands of the Midianites. " Then the Lord turned to him and said, "Go in this might of yours, and you shall save Israel from the hand of the Midianites. Have I not sent you?" So he said to Him, "O my Lord, how can I save Israel? Indeed, my clan is the weakest in Manasseh, and I am the least in my father's house." And the Lord said to him, "Surely I will be with you, and you shall defeat the Midianites as one man."

Then he said to Him, "If now I have found favour in Your sight, then show me a sign that it is You who talk with me. Do not depart from here,

I pray, until I come to You and bring out my offering and set it before You." And He said, "I will wait until you come back." So Gideon went in and prepared a young goat, and unleavened bread from an ephah of flour. The meat he put in a basket, and he put the broth in a pot; and he brought them out to Him under the terebinth tree and presented them. The Angel of God said to him, "Take the meat and the unleavened bread and lay them on this rock, and pour out the broth." And he did so. Then the Angel of the Lord put out the end of the staff that was in His hand, and touched the meat and the unleavened bread; and fire rose out of the rock and consumed the meat and the unleavened bread. And the Angel of the Lord departed out of his sight. Now Gideon perceived that He was the Angel of the Lord. So Gideon said, "Alas, O Lord God! For I have seen the Angel of the Lord face to face."

Samson's mother Manoah encountered Him. – Judges 13

Again, the children of Israel did evil in the sight of the Lord, and the Lord delivered them into the hand of the Philistines for forty years. Now there was a certain man from Zorah, of the family of the Danites, whose name was Manoah; and his wife was barren and had no children. And the Angel of the Lord appeared to the woman and said to her, "Indeed now, you are barren and have borne no children, but you shall conceive and bear a son. Now therefore, please be careful not to drink wine or similar drink, and not to eat anything unclean. For behold, you shall conceive and bear a son. And no razor shall come upon his head, for the child shall be a Nazirite to God from the womb; and he shall begin to deliver Israel out of the hand of the Philistines."

Joshua at the end of chapter Five, he encounters a stranger who tells him to take off his shoes for he's standing on a holy ground, and of course Joshua realises that reminds him of Moses' encounter in the burning bush some forty years earlier. This tells us that that has to be Jesus Christ.

How did Israel win the war against Jericho? It wasn't just the Music, it was the Lord Jesus Christ, and it's very important to understand because every rule of the Torah is violated by in the attack on Jericho. They didn't rest on the 7th day, they kept silent for six days and on the seventh day they shouted [A reverse of the sabbath rules]

When you start studying the conquest of Jericho in the book of Joshua, you'll discover carefully if you look that it's the outline of the book of revelation.

GABRIEL: He is one of the most frequently mentioned angels in the bible. He is a Messianic angel primarily; he is usually announcing something directly to do with the advent of the messiah both in the Old and New Testament.

He identifies as Gabriel in Luke 1:19 – I am Gabriel who stands In the presence of God.

And the angel answered and said to him, "I am Gabriel, who stands in the presence of God, and was sent to speak to you and bring you these glad tidings.

He was the Angel that was sent to Daniel to explain the vision of the ram and the he-goat as seen in Dan 8:16

And I heard a man's voice between the banks of the Ulai, who called, and said, "Gabriel, make this man understand the vision." So he came near where I stood, and when he came I was afraid and fell on my face; but he said to me, "Understand, son of man, that the vision refers to the time of the end.

In Daniel 9, He's the one who gave Daniel the fabled 70 weeks - Dan 9:21-27.

Yes, while I was speaking in prayer, the man Gabriel, whom I had seen in the vision at the beginning, being caused to fly swiftly, reached me about the time of the evening offering. And he informed me, and talked with me, and said, "O Daniel, I have now come forth to give you skill to understand. At the beginning of your supplications the command went out, and I have come to tell you, for you are greatly beloved; therefore consider the matter, and understand the vision: "Seventy weeks are determined. For your people and for your holy city, To finish the transgression, To make an end of sins, To make reconciliation for iniquity, To bring in everlasting righteousness, To seal up vision and prophecy, And to anoint the Most Holy. "Know therefore and understand, That from the going forth of the command To restore and build Jerusalem, Until Messiah the Prince, There shall be seven weeks and sixty-two weeks; The street shall be built again, and the wall, Even in troublesome times. "And after the sixty-two weeks, Messiah shall be cut off, but not for Himself; And the people of the prince who is to come, Shall destroy the city and the sanctuary. The end of it shall be with a flood, And till the end of the war desolations are determined. Then he shall confirm a covenant with many for one week; But in the middle of the week, He shall bring an end to sacrifice and offering. And on the wing of abominations shall be one who makes desolate, Even until the consummation, which is determined, Is poured out on the desolate."

He told Daniel the exact day the messiah would emerge to present Himself as King to Jerusalem and you'll find it in Luke 19 – The Triumphant entry

Gabriel announced the birth of John the Baptist - Lk 1:11

Then an angel of the Lord appeared to him, standing on the right side of the altar of incense.

Gabriel announced the Birth of the Messiah - Luke 1:26

Now in the sixth month the angel Gabriel was sent by God to a city of Galilee named Nazareth,

Gabriel is always announcing things. It will be an amazing title if we called him the press agent.

*Note that Gabriel never blows horns when he comes

CHERUBIM: The cherubim has four faces. One of the Cherubim turned bad, lucifer -The cherub that covereth – Ezekiel 28:14. He was in-charge of others but wanted to be equal with God. He got into trouble and took some lieutenants with him: Abaddon/ Apollyon: The destroyer

They are apparently some of his lieutenants under him but more powerful than the rest.

"The shape of the locusts was like horses prepared for battle. On their heads were crowns of something like gold, and their faces were like the faces of men. They had hair like women's hair, and their teeth were like lions' teeth. And they had breastplates like breastplates of iron, and the sound of their wings was like the sound of chariots with many horses running into battle. They had tails like scorpions, and there were stings in their tails. Their power was to hurt men five months. And they had as king over them the angel of the bottomless pit, whose name in Hebrew is Abaddon, but in Greek he has the name Apollyon.- Revelation 9:7-11

You might be wondering what the name Abaddon or Apollyon means and who they are. in Revelation 9:11, The Bible tells us that they had as king over them the angel of the Abyss, whose name in Hebrew is Abaddon, and in Greek, Apollyon." In Hebrew, the name "Abaddon" means "place of destruction"; the Greek title "Apollyon" literally means "The Destroyer."

Abaddon/Apollyon is the ruler of the Abyss and the king of these demonic locusts.

As we read through Revelation eight through nine, The Apostle John describes a period during the end times when angels sound seven trumpets. For each trumpet, it signified the coming of a new judgment on the people of earth. When the fifth angel blew his trumpet, the Abyss, a great smoking pit, will open, and a horde of demonic "locusts" will rise out of it As seen in Revelation 9:1-3.

These creatures will be given the power to torture any person who does not bear God's seal. The pain they inflict will be so intense that sufferers will wish to die.

Many scholars would usually use Abaddon/Apollyon as another name for Satan. However, the Bible seems to distinguish the two because we find Satan later on in Revelation when he is imprisoned for a thousand years during the millennium. He is then released to wreak havoc on the earth and ultimately receives his final, eternal punishment.

We can deduce that Abaddon/Apollyon is likely one of Satan's aide, a destroying demon and one of the "rulers," "authorities," and "powers" which the Apostle Paul mentions in Ephesians six.

Moreover the word of the Lord came to me, saying, "Son of man, take up a lamentation for the king of Tyre, and say to him, 'Thus says the Lord God:

"You were the seal of perfection,

Full of wisdom and perfect in beauty.

You were in Eden, the garden of God;

Every precious stone was your covering:

The sardius, topaz, and diamond,

Beryl, onyx, and jasper,

Sapphire, turquoise, and emerald with gold.

The workmanship of your timbrels and pipes

Was prepared for you on the day you were created.

"You were the anointed cherub who covers;

I established you;

You were on the holy mountain of God;

You walked back and forth in the midst of fiery stones.

 You were perfect in your ways from the day you were created,

Till iniquity was found in you.

"By the abundance of your trading

You became filled with violence within,

And you sinned;

Therefore I cast you as a profane thing

Out of the mountain of God;

And I destroyed you, O covering cherub,

From the midst of the fiery stones.

"Your heart was lifted up because of your beauty;

You corrupted your wisdom for the sake of your splendour;

I cast you to the ground,

I laid you before kings,

That they might gaze at you.

"You defiled your sanctuaries

By the multitude of your iniquities,

By the iniquity of your trading;

Therefore I brought fire from your midst;

It devoured you,

And I turned you to ashes upon the earth

In the sight of all who saw you.

All who knew you among the peoples are astonished at you;

You have become a horror,

And shall be no more forever." - Ezekiel 28:11-19

MICHAEL: He is a military leader on behalf of Israel

He is the Arch angel – Jude 1:9, 1 Thess. 4:16 where HE calls us to the rapture [The voice of the Arch Angel]. People ask what are we going to hear at the rapture, I tell them that they'll hear their names Just as Jesus calls Lazarus out of the Tomb!

"Yet Michael the archangel, in contending with the devil, when he disputed about the body of Moses, dared not bring against him a reviling accusation, but said, "The Lord rebuke you!"- Jude 1:9

For the Lord Himself will descend from heaven with a shout, with the voice of an archangel, and with the trumpet of God. And the dead in Christ will rise first. - 1 Thessalonians 4:16

He is one of the chief princes - Dan 10:13

But the prince of the kingdom of Persia withstood me twenty-one days; and behold, Michael, one of the chief princes, came to help me, for I had been left alone there with the kings of Persia

He is described as "your prince" - Dan 10:21.

But I will tell you what is noted in the Scripture of Truth. (No one upholds me against these, except Michael your prince.

He is an angelic leader specifically for the Jewish interest

In Daniel 12:1, he is the great prince that standeth for the children of thy people

"At that time Michael shall stand up, The great prince who stands watch over the sons of your people; And there shall be a time of trouble, Such as never was since there was a nation, Even to that time. And at that time your people shall be delivered, Every one who is found written in the book.

In Rev 12:7, there's a summary of the career of satan. In that chapter, there's a war in heaven and Michael and his angels fought against satan and his angels.

And war broke out in heaven: Michael and his angels fought with the dragon; and the dragon and his angels fought, - Revelation 12:7

However, there's something strange about Michael that raises a lot of allusion. When we come to the book of Jude, when Jude speaks of Apostasy [Verse 8-9]. Jude admonishes we should not speak against dignitaries but the example he used was one of the strangest one which was lucifer.

Michael was in a contest with Satan over the body of Moses, he did not rebuke Satan but said "the Lord rebuke you" and honestly, we don't know why and we don't know why Michael was fighting over the body of Moses because we saw Moses appear at the mount of transfiguration with Elijah and Jesus, and we also suspect for some reason that Moses will be one of the two witnesses that makes an appearance in Rev 11.

Another interesting reference is also in Zechariah 3

Then he showed me Joshua the high priest standing before the Angel of the Lord, and Satan standing at his right hand to oppose him. And the Lord said to Satan, "The Lord rebuke you, Satan! The Lord who has chosen Jerusalem rebuke you! Is this not a brand plucked from the fire?"- Zechariah 3:1-2

The Lord said to Satan "The Lord rebuke you, Satan!" it's fascinating that both Michael and this strange character here did not out rightly rebuke Satan, but used the name of the Lord to rebuke him. This is a great lesson for us too.

SUPER ANGELS

CHERUBIM

Have four wings, not just 2 as pictured.

- They guard the tree of life in Gen 3:24

So He drove out the man; and He placed cherubim at the east of the garden of Eden, and a flaming sword which turned every way, to guard the way to the tree of life.

- They adorn the mercy seat – Exo 25:10-22

"And they shall make an ark of acacia wood; two and a half cubits shall be its length, a cubit and a half its width, and a cubit and a half its height. And you shall overlay it with pure gold, inside and out you shall overlay it, and shall make on it a moulding of gold all around. You shall cast four rings of gold for it, and put them in its four corners; two rings shall be on one side, and two rings on the other side. And you shall make poles of acacia wood, and overlay them with gold. You shall put the poles into the rings on the sides of the ark, that the ark may be carried by them. The poles shall be in the rings of the ark; they shall not be taken from it. And you shall put into the ark the Testimony which I will give you. "You shall make a mercy seat of pure gold; two and a half cubits shall be its length and a cubit and a half its width. And you shall make two cherubim of gold; of hammered work you shall make them at the two ends of the mercy seat. Make one cherub at one end, and the other cherub at the other end; you shall make the cherubim at the two ends of it of one piece with the mercy seat. And the cherubim shall stretch out their wings above, covering the mercy seat with their wings, and they shall face one another; the faces of the cherubim shall be toward the mercy seat. You shall put the mercy seat on top of the ark, and in the ark you shall put the Testimony that I will give you. And there I will meet with you, and I will speak with you from above the mercy seat, from between the two cherubim which are on the ark of the Testimony, about everything which I will give you in commandment to the children of Israel.

These composite figures, exalted to be proximate to the dwelling place of God, they function in several ways:

They guard the ark in Solomon's temple in 1 King 6:23-28, 8:7

Inside the inner sanctuary he made two cherubim of olive wood, each ten cubits high. One wing of the cherub was five cubits, and the other wing of the cherub five cubits: ten cubits from the tip of one wing to the tip of the other. And the other cherub was ten cubits; both cherubim were of the same size and shape. The height of one cherub was ten cubits, and so was the other cherub. Then he set the cherubim inside the inner room; and they stretched out the wings of the cherubim so that the wing of the one touched one wall, and the wing of the other cherub touched the other wall. And their wings touched each other in the middle of the room. Also he overlaid the cherubim with gold.

They engage in the adoration of God in connection with the mercy seat in the tabernacle – Ex 25:18-20, 37:7-9

"And you shall make two cherubim of gold; of hammered work you shall make them at the two ends of the mercy seat. Make one cherub at one end, and the other cherub at the other end; you shall make the cherubim at the two ends of it of one piece with the mercy seat. And the cherubim shall stretch out their wings above, covering the mercy seat with their wings, and they shall face one another; the faces of the cherubim shall be toward the mercy seat".

"He made two cherubim of beaten gold; he made them of one piece at the two ends of the mercy seat: one cherub at one end on this side, and the other cherub at the other end on that side. He made the cherubim at the two ends of one piece with the mercy seat. The cherubim spread out their wings above, and covered the mercy seat with their wings. They faced one another; the faces of the cherubim were toward the mercy seat".

They support the Lord's throne – 1 Sam 4:3, 2 Sam 6:2, 2 Kings 19:15, Ps 80:1

"And when the people had come into the camp, the elders of Israel said, "Why has the Lord defeated us today before the Philistines? Let us bring the ark of the covenant of the Lord from Shiloh to us, that when it comes among us it may save us from the hand of our enemies."

"So they set the ark of God on a new cart, and brought it out of the house of Abinadab, which was on the hill; and Uzzah and Ahio, the sons of Abinadab, drove the new cart".

"Give ear, O Shepherd of Israel,

You who lead Joseph like a flock;

You who dwell between the cherubim, shine forth!"

They formed the chariots of deity when God moves – 2 Sam 22:11, PS 104:3, 1 Chr. 28:18

He rode upon a cherub, and flew; And He was seen upon the wings of the wind.

"He lays the beams of His upper chambers in the waters,

Who makes the clouds His chariot,

Who walks on the wings of the wind"

"And refined gold by weight for the altar of incense, and for the construction of the chariot, that is, the gold cherubim that spread their wings and overshadowed the ark of the covenant of the Lord".

Seraphim

Has six wings

Isaiah had a very key opportunity to see the throne of God and describes it in the book of Isaiah. In the Greek, especially in Revelation chapter 4 and 5, we encountered ZOON which is different from the beast in Revelation 13. which is the Greek term for *Living creatures* which was a vision John saw whilst he was at Patmos and he encounters these living creatures

We encountered these creatures only in Isaiah 6 but most likely the same in Revelation 4 :6-8 but with different names. They are there to celebrate the holiness of God and announce the trinity by saying "Holy Holy Holy"

IN Revelation 4, the living creatures are called Zoon but in Revelation 13, the word in the Greek in *therion* which means ferocious beast

As you read Ezekiel 1 -The Word "North" is idiomatically used to mean the throne of God – Isa 14:13, Ps 75:5-7.

"For you have said in your heart:

I will ascend into heaven,

I will exalt my throne above the stars of God;

I will also sit on the mount of the congregation

On the farthest sides of the north"

"Do not lift up your horn on high;

Do not speak with a stiff neck.'"

For exaltation comes neither from the east

Nor from the west nor from the south.

But God is the Judge:

He puts down one,

And exalts another"

We also see Satan aspires to be on that side of the north. I don't believe it's a geocentric term, I believe it is something larger.

Whenever we see the throne of God her in Ezekiel or Isaiah, it's always a source of Light, flames, fire – The very word seraphim implies that we see God as a consuming fire – Heb. 12:29, God is light – 1John 1:5, Paul at his conversion saw a light from Heaven. – Acts 26:13

Four living creatures – Ezekiel 1:5

Likeness is similar but not identical. It's not a synonym.

Likeness expresses a general form.

Likeness appears 10 times [Demuth]

appearance appears 14 times [Mareh]

Likeness and appearance are not the same, one is more specific than the other. The prophet senses the inadequacy of human speech to describe the ineffable [There's no way to express what he saw, he will only do the best that he can], I think this was Paul's frustration when he mentions the third heaven.

"It is doubtless not profitable for me to boast. I will come to visions and revelations of the Lord: I know a man in Christ who fourteen years ago— whether in the body I do not know, or whether out of the body I do not know, God knows—such a one was caught up to the third heaven. And I know such a man—whether in the body or out of the body I do not know, God knows— how he was caught up into Paradise and heard inexpressible words, which it is not lawful for a man to utter". - 2 Corinthians 12:1-4

These creatures symbolised the glory and power of God

"They turned not where they went" [Vs 9] – We know from James 1:17 that there is no variableness or turning. It's an optical term meaning absence of parallax which is mathematically the same thing as being at infinity. They could see in all directions and move in all directions without turning.

THE FOUR FACES BEFORE THE THRONE OF GOD

-Ezekiel 1, 10, Revelation 4, Numbers 2, The four gospels

1. Man
2. Lion
3. ox
4. Eagle

We discover the camp of Israel when laid out would organise itself around four camps. They are:

- Camp of Judah
- Camp of Ephraim
- Camp of Reuben
- Camp of Dan

When the camp of Israel was encamped in Numbers 2, according to the instruction if the Torah, they apparently at least in some sense were a model of the throne of God.

THE EASTERN CAMP – JUDAH

"All who were numbered according to their armies of the forces with Judah, one hundred and eighty-six thousand four hundred—these shall break camp first. - Numbers 2:9

THE SOUTHERN CAMP - REUBEN

"All who were numbered according to their armies of the forces with Reuben, one hundred and fifty-one thousand four hundred and fifty—they shall be the second to break camp. - Numbers 2:16

THE WESTERN CAMP - EPHRAIM

"All who were numbered according to their armies of the forces with Ephraim, one hundred and eight thousand one hundred—they shall be the third to break camp. - Numbers 2:24

THE NORTHERN CAMP - DAN

"All who were numbered of the forces with Dan, one hundred and fifty-seven thousand six hundred—they shall break camp last, with their standards."- Numbers 2:31

If we look at these numbers from these four camps from an aerial view, it takes the shape of a cross. The beauty of Numbers two is that it points to the cross. The creatures represented in numbers two was also a prophetic picture of the gospels.

These four faces also model the gospel:

1. Matthew – Lion of the Tribe of Judah
2. Mark – The suffering Servant Ox
3. Luke – Son of man
4. John – The Eagle

Matthew – Judah -East - Lion of the Tribe of Judah

Mark – Ephraim – West - The suffering Servant Ox

Luke – Reuben -South - Son of man

John – Dan -North - The Eagle

They seem to have a major significance, if nothing else but in the architecture of the bible itself.

"They turned not when they went" – God is moving forward without wavering, un-hesitantly towards the accomplishment of His purpose in this world today, nothing will deter God in what He has set His mind to accomplish, nothing can side-track Him could be the implication here.

Wings full of eyes – also in Pro 15:3- *The eyes of the Lord are in every place, - Proverbs 15:3*

Keeping watch on the evil and the good.

Picturing the omniscience of God as He rules His creation, and the movements of the wheels and the cherubim congruent.

THE MISCONCEPTIONS OF SATAN

We need to guard against the fables and distortions prevalent throughout the world's literature

Satan does not rule in Hell – Hell was created for him, it's his place of ultimate incarceration!

We use the word 'Hell" very loosely, we need to really recognise what it means.

In Greek, it's Hades, in Hebrew its Sheol. The idea of hell has its misconceptions in literatures which is quite a distance from the biblical perspectives.

The word Hell is an English word derived from the Saxon *helan*, which means "to cover; hence the covered or invisible place. In the scripture, there are four words that have translated in English as hell

Sheol, Hades, Gehanna and Tartarus

Sheol occurs 65 times in the Old Testament, it is derived from a root word which means to ask or demands; hence insatiableness – Proverbs 30:15,16

It is rendered Grave thirty-one times - Gen 37:35, 442:38, 44:29,31, 1Sam 2:6, et al.

However, let me say this here now that Grave and Sheol are quite different.

Sheol is rendered Hell thirty-one times as a place of disembodied spirits.

The inhabitants of sheol are the "congregation of the dead"

"The man that wandereth out of the way of understanding

shall remain in the congregation of the dead". - Proverbs 21:16

It is also the abode of the souls of the wicked dead in a number of places in the Bible

They, and all that appertained to them, went down alive into the pit, and the earth closed upon them: and they perished from among the congregation. - Numbers 16:33

Drought and heat consume the snow waters: so doth the grave those

The wicked shall be turned into hell, and all the nations that forget God. - which have sinned. - Job 24:19

It is also a place of the good that had passed

"For thou wilt not leave my soul in hell; neither wilt thou suffer thine Holy One to see corruption". - Psalms 16:10

"O Lord, thou hast brought up my soul from the grave: thou hast kept me alive, that I should not go down to the pit" - Psalms 30:3

"But God will redeem my soul from the power of the grave: for he shall receive me. Selah". - Psalms 49:15

"For great is thy mercy toward me: and thou hast delivered my soul from the lowest hell". - Psalms 86:13

Sheol is described as deep in job 11:8, dark in job 10:21,28, with bars in Job 17:16

"It is as high as heaven; what canst thou do? deeper than hell; what canst

thou know?" - Job 11:8

"They shall go down to the bars of the pit, when our rest together is in the dust". - Job 17:16

It is a place that the dead go down to as seen in Num. 16:30, 33,

"But if the Lord make a new thing, and the earth open her mouth, and swallow them up, with all that appertain unto them, and they go down" - Numbers 16:30

"They, and all that appertained to them, went down alive into the pit, and the earth closed upon them: and they perished from among the congregation". - Numbers 16:33

Sheol is not to be confused with the Grave. The Grave is called *Qeburah*. It is a different word in the Hebrew. Sometimes Sheol is used connotatively. However, the grave is a physical place for the bodies, not the disembodied spirits. You can own one or more graves, you can use grave in the plural but Sheol is never in the plural, it's always in the singular

The Greek equivalent term to grave is Hades. Hades is a Greek word for which is out of sight, to denote a place of the dead.

Hades is translated hell eleven times in the New Testament

The Septuagint *The Greek Translation of the Old Testament* uses hades to translate the Hebrew Sheol on sixty-one occasions – Gen 42:38, Psa. 139:8, Hos. 13:14, Isa 14:9

"And he said, My son shall not go down with you; for his brother is dead, and he is left alone: if mischief befall him by the way in the which ye go, then shall ye bring down my gray hairs with sorrow to the grave". - Genesis 42:38

"If I ascend up into heaven, thou art there: if I make my bed in hell,

behold, thou art there". - Psalms 139:8

"I will ransom them from the power of the grave;

I will redeem them from death:

O death, I will be thy plagues;

O grave, I will be thy destruction:

repentance shall be hid from mine eyes". - Hosea 13:14

"Hell from beneath is moved for thee to meet thee at thy coming: it stirreth up the dead for thee, even all the chief ones of the earth; it hath raised up from their thrones all the kings of the nations"- Isaiah 14:9

In Greek, it is associated with Orcus, the infernal regions, a dark and dismal place in the very depths of the earth, the common receptacle of all disembodied spirits.

In the Greek conceptions, it had two subterranean divisions: *Elysium and Tartarus*. That seems to parallel Luke 16. Elysium is a good place, which the paradise equivalent and Tartarus is the dark place.

Hades is referred to the abode of the unsaved dead prior to the great white throne judgement – Rev 20:11-15

Hades is a prison – 1 Peter 3:19

It has gates and bars and locks – Matthew 16:18, Rev 1:18

it is a downward concept in some sense – Matt 11:23, Lk 10:15

The righteous and the wicked are separated in hades

Some view the Blessed dead as in a part of Hades called Paradise – Luke 23:43

Hades is also alluded to as Abraham's bosom in Luke 16:22, we know that Abraham's bosom is regarded Heaven - Matt 8:11.

Most of the early church fathers regarded paradise as Heaven, not hades.

GEHENNA

It was originally *Ge bene Hinnom*, which was the valley of the sons of *Hinnom*. It was a city dump, which was a deep, narrow ravine to the south of Jerusalem separating Mount Zion from the so-called *"Hill of Evil counsel"*

We see from scripture that the idolatrous Jews offered their children in sacrifice of Molech in a very dark era of their time – 2Chro 28:3, 33:6, Jer. 7:31, 19:2-6

This valley afterwards became a city dump. A fire was continually burning there, so it becomes idiomatically the everlasting fire and burning and it is used in that sense Eleven times by the Lord Jesus Himself in Matt 5:22, 29,30 10:28, 18:9, 23:15, 33, Mk 9:43,45,47, Lk 12:5

There are differences between Hades and Gehenna, although both are translated "Hell" in the English but that causes confusion

Hades is temporary. Everything in Hades will ultimately be thrown into Gehenna in the end. – Rev 20:14

Gehenna is forever, it has no end, its outside the time dimension

Hades is in the earth, it appears to be geocentric in concept – Matt 12:40, it also seems to be associated with the bottomless pit - Abousso – The Abyss

There is a term we run into referred to as *"The Outer darkness"* in Matt 8:12, 22:13, 25:30 which is widely misunderstood by most people who haven't done their homework. This is to say that the outer darkness isn't Gehenna.

TARTARUS

This is another name translated as hell which only has one use in the New Testament – 2Pet 2:4

It is the specific place of incarceration of the angels that sinned - Gen 6, 2Pet 2:4, Jude 1:6 this is for the fallen angels that sinned but gets released in a very strange way in Revelation apparently.

ABOUSSO

This is another term referred to as the *bottomless pit*. This is where the beast of revelation 11:7-8 emerge from. It is also a place that Satan would be bound for a thousand years as seen in Rev 20:1-3. This is also a place from which the demon locust emerge in Revelation 9.

These collectively is called the underworld and Hades is the collective Greek term for it.

There is an impassable gulf between Abraham's bosom and the place of torment

Luke 16 is not a parable, it's an actual event

The man in Hades was fully conscious –

- He had a memory, he was speaking, he was in deep pain, he had desires
- His eternal destiny was irrevocably fixed
- He knew what he was experiencing was fair and just
- He also knew his brothers needed to do to avoid his own fate: repent.

- He was not yet in hell; he was in hades – Gehenna is yet future on his situation

When Jesus goes to the cross, spends three days in the grave, He goes down there to declare his victory, then He gathered those in Abraham's bosom to be with Him from that point on – So He emptied that section of hades. – 1Pet 3:19

MISCONCEPTIONS

Satan does not rule in Hell, Hell was created for him

There are two prevalent myths about satan

1. That he doesn't exist – People think it's just a collective term for evil. No! he is a person; he has a personality. He has an origin and he has a destiny.

2. He has locality – he is not omnipresent but his resources are enormous and substantial

EZEKIEL 28

Ethbaal III was removed from his throne by Nebuchadnezzar in 573 – 572 BC in the 6th century. The prince of Tyre [nagid] is the first eleven verses. He was an actual prince.

The King of Tyre [Melek] from verse 11-19

There is a shifting scope. The passage will go beyond the person sitting on the throne to the power behind the throne. The Language, though primarily here applied to the King of Tyre, is similar language to the King of Babylon - Isa 14, yet has an ulterior and fuller accomplishment in satan and his embodiment in the antichrist – Dan7:25, 2Thess 2:4, Rev 13:6

In verse thirteen of Ezekiel 28, The precious stones are the same stones we find on the breastplate of high priests.

The first [Sardius] – Reuben "Behold a son" and The twelfth [Jasper] – Benjamin "son of my righthand'

Nine of twelve are mentioned -Ex 39:10-13, Rev 21:14, 19-21

The tambourines and pipes suggest that he was built for worship.

He was a cherub [super Angel] - Isa 6, Ezekiel 1&10, Rev 4& 5.

Satan as well as the angels were created before the foundation of the earth They rejoiced when God laid the foundation. Christ created satan, He used the logos to create everything, including satan

Ezekiel described the king in terms that could not be a mere man.

This king:

- Appeared in the garden of Eden – vs 13
- Had been a guardian cherub – vs 14a
- Had possessed free access to God's Holy mountains - vs 14b
- Had been sinless from the time he was created – vs 15

ISAIAH 14

Isaiah 14 gives us a similar glimpse about the origin of satan. This is lamentation of the king of Babylon, but it goes way beyond Babylon

"Fallen from heaven" with the famous five "I wills" here [Verse 13,14]

For thou hast said in thine heart,

1. I will ascend into heaven,
2. I will exalt my throne above the stars of God:
3. I will sit also upon the mount of the congregation, in the sides of

the north:

4. I will ascend above the heights of the clouds;
5. I will be like the most High.

- His origin is mentioned in Ezekiel 28 and Isaiah 14
- His agenda is summarised in Revelation 12
- His destiny in detailed in Rev 20 and 21
- Satan is an actual person, he's not some kind of force or personification of evil
- He has intelligence – Job 1:6-12
- He has emotion – Rev 12:12-17
- He has volition – 2 Tim 2:26
- He was created and was originally very goods - Gen 1:31
- He was created by Christ for him – Col 1:16
- Yet sometime after his creation before Genesis 3, he rebelled against God and lost his holy condition, through conceit.
- He is a fallen angel obviously as seen in Matt 25:41, Rev 12:7-8
- After his fall, he led both angels and human beings into spiritual death by his murderous, untruthful schemes – John 8:44.
- We discovered from Revelation 12 that one third of the Angels rebelled with satan - Rev 12:4
- He's spoken as the prince of this world – John 12:31, 14:30, 16:11
- He's the god of this age – 2 Cor 4:4

- He's the prince of the power of the air – Ephesians 2:2
- He is the evil one – Matt 13:19
- He is the enemy – Matt 13:39
- He is a murderer, liar, father of lies – John 8:44
- He's called the tempter - Matt 4:3, 1 Thessalonians 3:6
- He's an adversary like a roaring lion – 1Peert 5:8
- He's spoken of as the great dragon who deceives the whole world – Rev 12:9
- He is the ancient serpent – 2Cor 11:3, Rev 20:2
- He can appear as angel of light – 2Cor 11:14
- He's referred to as Beelzebub in Matt 12:24-27
- He's known as Belial in 2Cor 6:15
- He has his own kingdom – Luke 11:17-20
- The whole world is under the control of the evil one – 1Jn 5:19
- His powers are great, yet he is not all powerful
- He is able to affect the processes of nature, so to cause even physical death – Ex 7:10-12
- He is not omnipotent – Ex 8:18, 9:11, Rev 12:7-9
- He needs God's permission to do what he does – job 1:12, 2:6, Lk 8:12, 22:31

- He is extremely wise. – Ephesians 6:11, Rev 12:9 but not omniscient – Job 1:11, 21-11
- He travels rapidly around the world – job 1:1 but he is not omnipresent – Matt 4:11
- He has great influence in the affairs of human government – John 12:31, yet his forces are not invincible. – Dan 10:12-14

There is a summary of him in revelation 12 where we have the imagery of the woman and the man-child

We have the woman – **ISRAEL**

who was identified with the sun, moon and 12 stars, She is in a predicament because she's with child

We also have a red dragon that tried to attack her - **SATAN**

He has 7 heads, 10 horns and 7 crowns

Satan's mission is to devour the man child when born

We have the Man-Child – **KINSMAN REDEEMER**

He rules all the nations with a rod of iron

He is caught up to God and His throne

The woman flees into the wilderness for 1260 days

Michael and his angels fight the Dragon and his angels

The Dragon is cast to the earth and the devil persecutes the woman for three and a half years

Let's be clear that the woman is not the Church, she is an idiom of Israel. The Church cannot be pregnant!

God expelled satan from the mount of God [Heaven] – Ezekiel 28:16

He was cast from God's government in Heaven [Job 1:6-12] but was till allowed access to God – [Zechariah 3:1-2]

In the tribulation, satan will be cast from heaven and restricted to the earth. -Rev 12:7-8

During the millennium, he'll be confined to the bottomless pit – Rev 20:1-3

The two beasts will be cast into Gehenna but satan will be incarcerated and after his release at the end of the millennium, he leads another rebellion and will be cast into the lake of fire forever – Rev 20:10

The locusts of Revelation 9 had. King over them – the angel of the abyss, whose name in Hebrew is Abaddon and Apollyon in the Greek.

Some people these are just similar titles of satan

There's also the locus of Amos 7 which had a king over them - A leader by the name of Gog – Amos 7:1 [LXX] – Ezekiel 38-39, you'll be dealing with a demonic title

THE HYBRIDS

IN Genesis 6, the first two verses are one sentence

The word "sons of God" is referred to as Bene Ha Elohim which means direct creation of God [This could be only Adam and the Angels]

The daughters of men is a different term known as Benoth Adam – Daughters of Adam.

This is a term of Angels in the Old Testament [Job 1:6, 2, 38:7]

This is also used in the New Testament [Luke 20:36]

The Nephilim were the outcome of the strange union between the sons of God and the daughters of man. Keep in mind that the Nephilim was not just before the flood of Noah but also after that as seen in Genesis 6

*"There were giants in the earth in those days; **and also after that**, when the sons of God came in unto the daughters of men, and they bare children to them, the same became mighty men which were of old, men of renown". - Genesis 6:4*

The word in the Hebrew is Nephilim which means the fallen ones, which comes a Hebrew word "Nephal" meaning to cast away, desert.

In Genesis 6:9, the word perfect is Tamiym in the Greek which means without blemish, sound, healthy, without spot, unimpaired. This means that Noah's family was not corrupted by the mixture of these hybrids that satan had introduced.

Many people have confusion about angels and sex.

Jesus tells us two places in the New Testament that angels in Heaven not getting married, etc [Matt 22:30, Mk 12:25]

This is in reference to angels that are in heaven, not the fallen ones.

We do know that when angels appear on the earth, they are usually male.

There is another word in the New Testament that was used twice – *Oiketerion* in the Greek which means habitation or the body as a dwelling place for the spirit. It is from which the angels who fell had disrobed – Jude `1:6

It is also alluded to the heavenly body that the believer longs to be clothed – 2 Cor 5:2

For in this we groan, earnestly desiring to be clothed upon with our house which is from heaven: - 2 Corinthians 5:2

Let's take a look at the post flood Nephilim

"Also after that" …. Genesis 6:4

There are 4 tribes we find in Genesis 14 and 15 [Rephaim, Emim, Horim and Zamzummim] which apparently were bad news because Joshua is told to wipe them off. When you get to Numbers 13:33, we discovered Arba, Anak and seven sons. These Anakites were also giants. They were Nephilim, in fact the spies announced on their return that there were Nephilim in the land

We also see Og, King of Bashan in Deuteronomy 3:11 and Joshua 12 who was a Nephilim. We also see Goliath and his four brothers

DEMONS

In Daniel 10, we realised that spiritual conflicts occur among spiritual beings behind the emergence of major empires. This angel had to fight through the resistance of the Persian empire to get through and also announced to fight Greece later, even though Greece was two centuries later.

We also learnt that these spirit beings are territorial and they have locality. These spirit beings impact and are impacted by own actions.

We see all kinds of caricatures about Satan, most of them quite frivolous, but in addition, a huge body of literatures like "The Divine Comedy" which was an epic poem written by Dante Alighieri in 1308 and his death in 1321. His classic was widely considered the preeminent work of Italian literature and is seen as one of the greatest works of world literature. On the surface, the poem describes Dante's travels through the medieval concepts of hell, purgatory and Heaven: allegorically it represents a soul's journey towards God but the sad thing was that Dante draws on medieval Christian theology and philosophy, especially Thomistic philosophy and the Summa Theologica of Thomas Aquinas.

Another one to consider is Faust, who is the protagonist of a classic German legend. He was a highly successful scholar but also dissatisfied with his life, makes a deal with the devil, exchanging his soul for unlimited knowledge and worldly pleasure. His tale is the basis for many literary, artistic, cinematic, and musical works. Faust's name was used as an adjective Faustian which is used to describe an arrangement in which an ambitious person surrenders moral integrity in order to achieve power and success, which was a proverbial "date with the devil". His comic puppet was popular in Germany in the 16th century, but was popularized in England in his play, Tragical History of Doctor Faustus.

These ideas pervade our literatures in many forms but they tend to form a presumption about Satan that's incorrect.

Going as early as Genesis 3 *"And I will put enmity Between you and the woman, And between your seed and her Seed; He shall bruise your head, And you shall bruise His heel."*. That prophetic word of God starts a warfare between two seeds.

The seed of the woman which is a title of the Messiah, Jesus Christ

The seed of the serpent which is the adversary.

Many people don't realise that just as there was a messiah on the good side, there is an evil one called the seed of the servant, which of course is the adversary. these are the forces that lie behind the entire biblical scenario. These same forces are behind the world power today. All these will lead to a climax, which is the coming of the world ruler, which we popularly call the anti-Christ who will have a false prophet… But that is eschatology and we don't want to hammer that on this book as our main focus is on Angels and demons.

Demons are not the same thing as Angels. We must understand their limitations and agendas. They are not just idioms for psychiatric illusions, they are real beings.

Although in Matthew's account they mentioned they had a destiny but it was too soon for Jesus to damn them. The fact that they have a knowledge of their destiny is provocative. They identified Jesus and was aware of their destiny. This was not a psychiatric conjecture.

The east side of the sea of Galilee. It's a gentile area that was why there were swine. It was part of the Decapolis.

But why they did ask for permission to be cast into the swine and most importantly why did Jesus grant their desires? I believed Jesus did so to show to us that demons are real and it's not an allusion or hallucination of the demoniac.

That's a lot of demons!

The demons recognised and announced His deity. They announced what was not known at that time. They also knew their destiny and that Jesus has control over this.

Demons are different from fallen angels. Fallen angels can materialise but demons can't.

Demons are under satan's control. They are some of his resources. They are malevolent. They are dangerous, and if you are not a Christian you are vulnerable to them.

They are not simply some kind of psychiatric disorder. Someone who is properly trained in psychiatric will note the difference and deal with them accordingly.

They could not indwell animals without permission.

Demons are powerless without a host body. They are always seeking embodiment and when they have a host, they have a super human strength. They have a destiny. Some people suspect that they are the disembodies Nephilim – we know that the hybrids were formed in Genesis 6 and they drowned in the flood but what happened to the bodies of the Nephilim in the flood? Because of this, we suspect that the demons are the spirits of disembodied Nephilim, however that's a speculation as there's no way to nail that biblically.

The demons need an entry to inhabits human and we grant them most times of our own volition, that's why certain kinds of practices are dangerous because we can open doors for entries. Lowering the gate can be dangerous and we must understand that demons want access. Things like occult practices, role-playing games: Seances, false worship, etc.

Demons have zones of influence.

What does the Golan heights, Hebron and the Gaza strip have in common geographically?

They were the areas that Joshua failed to exterminate the Raphaim in Deuteronomy 20:16-18, Jos 15:14, etc

"But of the cities of these people, which the Lord thy God doth give thee for an inheritance, thou shalt save alive nothing that breatheth: But thou shalt utterly destroy them; namely, the Hittites, and the Amorites, the Canaanites, and the Perizzites, the Hivites, and the Jebusites; as the Lord thy God hath commanded thee: That they teach you not to do after all their abominations, which they have done unto their gods; so should ye sin against the Lord your God". - Deuteronomy 20:16-18

There were 4 tribes he was instructed to wipe out every one of a certain tribe. When you read that as a New Testament reader, you would be shocked but Joshua didn't quite finish in certain areas. If you do a study of Joshua and judges, you'll notice that there are certain strongholds that Israel failed to defeat completely and they were the Golan, the area called the west bank and Gaza. In fact, Jericho means *the house of the moon god.*

When Jesus was hung on the cross as seen in Psalm 22:12

What are Bulls there in this scripture?

It could be used of men, angels, animals

It is also a metaphor of enemies, princes, objects.

It could be demon hosts surrendering the cross during His ordeal!

DEMONOLOGY

We hear the word "demons" here and there, actually the word is not a church word. Demon is an English translation if the word Daimon, which Is a spirit being. There are many theological divides as to where they came from. There are three major players as to where these beings came from. In all of these, I can confidently say that God did not create them. However I agree they are spirits of disembodied beings. *To declare that the Lord is upright; He is my rock, and there is no unrighteousness in Him. - Psalms 92:15*

There's a position that believes they are fallen angels, there's another position that believes they are spirits from the pre-adamic race and a final thought which believes they are spirits from the disembodies nephilims. We are not certain which is true from these different camps. Although important but the whole idea of this book is to identify them and CAST them out! Whilst this is not a theological resource which argues for their origin, we know their end. We know they have a destiny in hell.

Demonology is the study of demons and it's quite complicated because of the many conjectures that's been passed over the years and without any thorough biblical investigation, we have adapted a misinformed position on demons.

For one, I am not in agreement with the majority view who believe that demons are fallen Angels. Looking at the grammar and translation in scripture, their Hebraic and Greek rendering did not change from Bene H'Elohim [Sons of God] to Daimonion. There are three sons of God used in the scripture and this term often refers to God's direction creation. They include The Angels, Adam and of course you and I when we become born again. Even though fallen because of disobedience, their identity didn't change to become earth bound demons!

We are clear on fallen angels, but there's nothing in scripture which verify that there were derivatives from these fallen angels. There is no place in the bible that makes the earth the domain of Angels and there's no place that demons are in the heavenlies. This is to say that fallen angels are not resident in the earth.

Sadly, our English language do not have the capacity to capture the meaning of Daimon. Daimon is a noun and has an adjective derivative called daimonion which has become a noun to mean demons in the English translation. May I suggest that there is no place in scripture which suggests that angels desire to possess man or things but we find demons in the bible begging to even possess swine. Effective deliverance comes from knowledge and as mentioned, this is not to prove a point theologically but present information so we know how to pray. Nowhere in the bible that instructs us to wrestle with demons but to cast it out. However, in Ephesians six, Paul commends we wrestle against heavenly beings. Isn't this interesting? Could there be something we need to press in to see?

Another confusion we find especially in the KJV is using the word "Devils". There is no plurality of devils. There's only one devil and many demons.

Devil in the Greek is diabolos as singular, so pluralizing the devil is a misrepresentation of devil. As we proceed, I'll also address the idea about "demon Possession". Can demons really possess Christ's property?

Should possession be used or subjected to demonic influence? I think the latter best suggests the verb "daimonizo"

Finally, my brethren, be strong in the Lord and in the power of His might. Put on the whole armour of God, that you may be able to stand against the wiles of the devil. For we do not wrestle against flesh and blood, but against principalities, against powers, against the rulers of the darkness of this age, against spiritual hosts of wickedness in the heavenly places- Ephesians 6:10-12

Principalities, powers, rulers of darkness and spiritual hosts of wickedness.... Where? IN THE HEAVENLY PLACES!!! All these are ranks of Angels mentioned and not ranks of demons when used in the right context.

Then they went into Capernaum, and immediately on the Sabbath He entered the synagogue and taught. And they were astonished at His teaching, for He taught them as one having authority, and not as the scribes. Now there was a man in their synagogue with an unclean spirit. And he cried out, saying, "Let us alone! What have we to do with You, Jesus of Nazareth? Did You come to destroy us? I know who You are— the Holy One of God!" But Jesus rebuked him, saying, "Be quiet, and come out of him!" And when the unclean spirit had convulsed him and cried out with a loud voice, he came out of him. Then they were all amazed, so that they questioned among themselves, saying, "What is this? What new doctrine is this? For with authority He commands even the unclean spirits, and they obey Him." And immediately His fame spread throughout all the region around Galilee. - Mark 1:21-28 (NKJV)

This possibly could be a leader in the synagogue or a regular consistent member of that synagogue and perhaps nobody knew he was under demonic influence, but before we look at the text critically, the bible says they were astonished at His teaching, for He taught them as one having authority, and not as the scribes.

Let's work on this text for a moment!

Jesus taught as one having authority, not as the scribes; This means that the scribes were readers and not exemplars of the texts. They know how to recite what was in the scrolls but did not operate in power. This is interesting to know because this is what many seminaries are like today. They know how to theoretically build theological names for things but don't understand the spiritual implications thereof. They knew about demons but don't understand the power to cast them out. They would use magic and incantations to try exorcising demons. Jesus hadn't even casted out the demons yet when they affirmed he taught with authority. This is good because not only was his demonstration with authority but His information too. He taught with authority, he'll cast the demon with authority too. This is a model of good homiletic teaching. Our teaching must be with authority, not like the scribes!

According to the text, the people there were already amazed at his authoritative teaching and now they are about to witness something that has never been done!

Perhaps this was the first time to ever witness such disturbance in the synagogue because this was the first time someone had taught with authority. If you look closely, it was the demon who couldn't contain himself. Jesus didn't go to him and lay hands on him but the demon couldn't stand the power of God. I have always believed that deliverance is deliberate and I am right with this.

The demon was not leaving the man just yet but the demon was confronting Jesus and trying to announce Jesus' mission as a way of exposing Jesus before His time, so Jesus quieted the demon. Jesus did two things

1. Quieted the demon because He didn't want the demon to ruin His timing
2. He Exorcised the demon.

The point I'm making here is that when the demons was exorcised, they were all amazed, so that they questioned among themselves, saying, "What is this? What new doctrine is this? For with authority He commands even the unclean spirits, and they obey Him.

They didn't question Him, they questioned amongst themselves by asking three questions:

1. What is this?
2. For with authority He commands even the unclean spirits?
3. For with authority He commands even the unclean spirits, and they obey Him?

What is this?

They have never seen this ever happen before. They questioned everything from His teaching to the demonic convulsion

For with authority He commands even the unclean spirits?

They had only exorcised demons with spells, magic, sorcery or other incantations. They have never seen anyone cast out demons without any of those means and they asked with what authority He did that.

For with authority He commands even the unclean spirits, and they obey Him?

I guess it's more like saying "Who's this dude that even unclean spirits obey Him?"

This made his fame spread abroad but it wasn't the demon who spread his name, it's His authority. Remember He quieted the demons but didn't quiet the people around.

It's interesting to see that demons know him and the people around didn't even know Him as the Holy One of God.

It is noteworthy to also make it clear that Jesus did not cast the man, He casted the spirit

This also reminds me of the Philippi encounter when Paul and his guys were approached by a damsel with a python spirit… let's look at this scripture and pick up some points too. This is an interesting one because here we see a sly spirit, a demon who pretended to be on Paul's side but exposed this false evil spirit and exorcised it.

However, what comes to mind is that it took a while for Paul to act on this cunning spirit but when he eventually had to deal with it, he dealt with it very well.

Now it happened, as we went to prayer, that a certain slave girl possessed with a spirit of divination met us, who brought her masters much profit by fortune-telling. This girl followed Paul and us, and cried out, saying, "These men are the servants of the Most High God, who proclaim to us the way of salvation." And this she did for many days.

But Paul, greatly annoyed, turned and said to the spirit, "I command you in the name of Jesus Christ to come out of her." And he came out that very hour. - Acts 16:16-18

The very first word I'd like to address is the word "Possessed" which is an unfortunate mistranslation for "Daimonizo". Daimonizo as a verb has nothing in the English meaning referring to possession but Oppression or subject to demonic influence. She was under demonic influence of the python spirit. In today's church verbiage, we call this the "serpentine spirit" because of its cunning nature. It was so sly that Paul was unable to discern quickly its pretentious nature. She was under the serpentine spirit of craftiness and cunningness and she did this to her victims by fortune telling. Fortune telling is one of the occultic practices, the others being divination and extrasensory procedure.

Fortune telling was a way she extorted money from her victims, the idea is that she would predict via divination but she appears very sly. The devil chose his right candidate – a damsel!

The interesting thing here is that she didn't come confronting them but was in a way, you would almost think she was helping them evangelise. *"These men are the servants of the Most High God, who proclaim to us the way of salvation"*. Looking at this, you'd wonder why the demon is making such announcement and not confront them. Actually, if you look at it spiritually and critically, I believe the serpent spirit was deliberate about this. As she spoke, I could literally feel the demon with venoms poisoning the minds and hearts of the people. I could imagine Paul and his crew trying to evangelise but was unable to win any soul for the Lord because this serpent spirit would have poisoned their minds with venom.

And this she did for many days.

And I can imagine Paul saying to his guys after some days "Guys, what's going on? We haven't been able to witness to anyone successfully, do we have a mole?" I can almost hear Paul say "something is wrong and we need to deal with this as soon as possible because it's been 4 days now and we haven't won a single soul"

But Paul, greatly annoyed, turned and said to the spirit, "I command you in the name of Jesus Christ to come out of her." And he came out that very hour

Paul was "greatly annoyed". That word in the Greek is diaponeomai meaning to be displeased, grieved, offended, pained. Paul was so annoyed that he "turned". The word turn doesn't necessarily mean to physically turn, it means to come back to one's senses and the word used is "Epistrepho". In my opinion, Paul did not use discernment until now and now he came back to reality that their unsuccessful mission could have been because he allowed her in their adventure. Paul commanded the demon to come out of the damsel and "he" came out that very hour. It's important that demons have a neuter gender but always presented in the masculine form. We see this also in Genesis 3 where the scripture called the devil "And he said to the woman...."

Just as Jesus didn't cast the man away from Church but the demon from the man, so we are also admonished to cast demons from people and not people from the Church!

There's something I'd also like to clear out when Jesus exorcised the demon from the man we read from in Mark 1. The bible said *when the unclean spirit had convulsed him and cried out with a loud voice, he came out of him.* I want to make it clear that the man did not convulse the demon but the demon convulsed the man. This is to say that convulsion is not a compulsory sign of successful exorcism. We don't shake demons out, we cast them out!

Exorcism wasn't new to the Jewish people but they were amazed because Jesus had exorcised a demon with another kind of procedure, they questioned this amongst themselves and would eventually confront Jesus with this question by saying He did this by Beelzebub. Let's follow up in Matthew 12.

"Then one was brought to Him who was demon-possessed, blind and mute; and He healed him, so that the blind and mute man both spoke and saw. And all the multitudes were amazed and said, "Could this be the Son of David?" Now when the Pharisees heard it they said, "This fellow does not cast out demons except by Beelzebub, the ruler of the demons." But Jesus knew their thoughts, and said to them: "Every kingdom divided

against itself is brought to desolation, and every city or house divided against itself will not stand. If Satan casts out Satan, he is divided against himself. How then will his kingdom stand? And if I cast out demons by Beelzebub, by whom do your sons cast them out? Therefore they shall be your judges. But if I cast out demons by the Spirit of God, surely the kingdom of God has come upon you. Or how can one enter a strong man's house and plunder his goods, unless he first binds the strong man? And then he will plunder his house. He who is not with Me is against Me, and he who does not gather with Me scatters abroad". - Matthew 12:22-30

They called Jesus a fellow and said he casted out demons by Beelzebub. They have accused him of using the power of Beelzebub to exorcise demons and Jesus asked them a very important question and asked them to be a judge over the question. *"And if I cast out demons by Beelzebub, by whom do your sons cast them out? Therefore they shall be your judges"* Here Jesus asked them in a nutshell "If you accuse me of doing this wrongly, then your sons would be doing it right – Therefore by what means do your sons cast out demons?" This question Jesus asked them would make them agree that Jesus did cast out demons like their sons but they were not willing to agree because they were looking for ways to hold him down, but Jesus didn't end there.

He then gave them the answer because He knew they don't even have an idea what they were saying. He said to them ". *But if I cast out demons by the Spirit of God, surely the kingdom of God has come upon you"* He gave them the answer to their question about authority. He said to them a Kingdom divided against itself cannot stand, meaning these demons leave these people because I am working against this demonic kingdom and if I am against this kingdom of darkness then I do this with the authority in the Kingdom of God. The kingdom of God has come upon you. So I do not need your orthodox exorcism practice to cast demons out but with the power of God. If we look closely at what Jesus was really saying, He was saying these magic, sorcery, divination and other incantations do not exorcise demons because demonic powers cannot work against demonic influences. This means that those Jewish exorcists don't really cast out demons, the demons only pretend to leave the people only to torment them much more.

There's never a place where a kingdom divided against itself ever stood but Jesus came to reveal another kingdom and He let them know the kingdom of God has come upon them!

We cast out demons by the power of God and not by any other means. It's the kingdom of God against the kingdom of satan.

CLOSING REMARK

Thank you for taking the time to flip through and scroll through the pages of this work, it is my prayer that you come to grasp the awesomeness of our God and our king in whom we believe as the creator of creation and creatures! And I leave you with this closing:

"The grace of the Lord Jesus Christ, and the love of God, and the communion of the Holy Spirit be with you all. Amen" -2Cor 13:14

Printed in Great Britain
by Amazon